Christmas HAIKU

PATRICIA FURSTENBERG

Text Copyright © Patricia C Furstenberg 2017

Patricia C Furstenberg asserts the moral right to be identified as the author of this work.

All rights reserved. No part of this publication may be reproduced, distributed, down-loaded, stored or transmitted in any form or by any means, including photocopying, recording, or other electronical and mechanical methods, without the prior written permission of the author.

Print Edition ISBN 9781790602674
Version: 2018-11-29
First print edition 2018
Cover Design: Patricia Furstenberg
Independently Published

Other books by Patricia Furstenberg

The Cheetah and the Dog
The Elephant and the Sheep
The Lion and the Dog

Puppy, 12 Months of Rhymes and Smiles
As Good as Gold
Belle Cat

Joyful Trouble
Happy Friends

Jock of the Bushveld
Huberta the Hippo
Vonk the Horse

Connect with the author on Twitter: @PatFurstenberg
Author's website: www.alluringcreations.co.za/wp

For Mom and Dad

CONTENTS

1 December - Snowflake

2 December - Chestnuts

3 December - Family

4 December - Gingerbread Man

5 December - Icicle

6 December - Christmas Tree

7 December - Candle Light

8 December - Happy

9 December - Lights

10 December - Nutcracker

11 December - Hope

12 December - Sleigh

15 December - Mistletoe

16 December - Joy

17 December - Angel

18 December - Cookies

19 December - Bells

20 December - Candy cane

21 December - Blizzard

22 December - Carolers

23 December - Jesus

24 December - Christmas Eve

25 December - 1st day of Christmas

26 December - 2nd day of Christmas

27 December - 3nd day of Christmas

28 December - 4th day of Christmas

29 December - 5th day of Christmas

30 December - 6th day of Christmas

31 December - 7th day of Christmas

1st January - 8th day of Christmas

2nd January - 9th day of Christmas

3rd January - 10th day of Christmas

4th January - 11th day of Christmas

5th January - 12th day of Christmas

1st December - *Snowflake*

It falls, slides with joy

A dream? Longed for, urged, wished, hoped!

Winter's first present.

2 December – Chestnuts

Without their prickles

Chestnuts crackle in fire.

Fingers icy red.

3 December – Family

Small hands, wrinkled hands

Share the same crooked smile and nose.

Photo of my heart.

4 December - Gingerbread Man

Flour and smarties,

To build winter's first snowman.

Sparrow's Christmas lunch.

5 December – Icicle

Drip, drip, drip outside.

Icicle, nature's sculpture.

En garde, pussy cat!

6 December - Christmas Tree

So tall for small child,

Only Dad reaches its top.

Christmas tree promise.

7 December – Candlelight

Enchanting secret

Scattered around, never lost.

A shared dream lives on.

8 December - Happy

Town sleeps covered by

freshly sieved snow. Sun smiles bright.

Red bird hops around.

9 December –Lights

Shimmers in the tree

Red, green, yellow, blue - thy blink.

My smile reflects you.

10 December – Nutcracker

Walnuts, hazelnuts

He cracks most, yet loves almonds,

En pointe, like Clara.

11 December – Hope

Winter's snow brings hope

Of fish in pond and new crops.

Swallows with twin eggs.

12 December – Sleigh

A joyride through snow;

Santa glides across the sky.

A winter's night dream.

13 December – Star

Brighter than the moon

In its magical glory.

Prayer for my home.

14 December – Snowball

Childhood's snowball fight

To the beat of my young heart.

Winters of my life.

16 December – Joy

Christmas morning sun

Shines on bows and presents. Joy!

My first coffee cup.

17 December - Angel

Fashioned, knitted, bought,

He spreads good will, blessing all.

Angel atop tree

18 December – Cookies

Christmas, snow, giggles,

Young and old around the tree.

Scent of fresh cookies.

19 December – Bells

Ding-dong, chimes for all,

Penniless, wealthy, young, old.

Silver bells in tree.

20 December – Candy cane

White, red, strips of joy

Sticky fingers, gluey smile

Long lost memory.

21 December – Blizzard

My joy in thy breath.

From white clouds wind blows,

Blizzard around, white temple.

22 December – Carolers

Voices in the night

Joy and stars spark across town.

Tears in my eyes.

23 December – Jesus

Holy child, God's gift

Wrapped in hay, guarded by sheep.

White dove glides above.

24 December – Christmas Eve

A star shines brighter,

Yearly promise of hope.

Last unwrapped present.

25 December – 1st day of Christmas

Partridge in pear tree

Feathers fly around, chirping.

I contemplate snow.

26 December – 2nd day of Christmas

Fluffed up and coo-ing,

Two turtle doves dance tango.

Bright blue sky above.

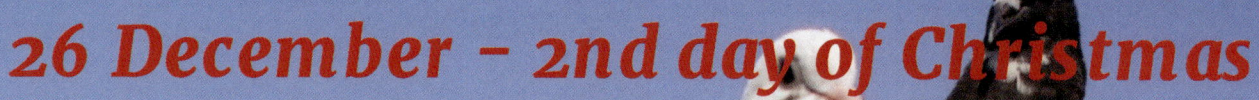

27 December – 3rd Day of Christmas

Three salmon shade hens

Dance. Feathered feet, ten toes each.

A bright green worm stretched.

28 December – 4th Day of Christmas

Thick necks, black, shaggy

Feathers, raven's high shrill warns:

Fear! Four calling birds.

29 December – 5th Day of Christmas

Circle of promise

Written in gold, forever.

Five rings mugger's luck.

30 December – 6th Day of Christmas

Webbed feet, menace honk,

Orange bill, wings spread out. Run!

Still lake at sunset.

31st December – 7th Day of Christmas

Plumed water lily

Gliding shyly away. Swan.

Odette, not Odile.

1st January – 8th Day of Christmas

Hay on the shed's floor,

Steamy, barny-odor milk.

Last star shies away.

2nd January – 9th Day of Christmas

Nine gowns a' dancing

One, two, spin; three, four and round.

None flowers swaying.

3rd January - 10th Day of Christmas

On pouring days when

Sky and earth by rain are joined -

Leap frog games indoors.

4th January - 11th Day of Christmas

Graceful tartan plaids

With auld bag pipes and wee drums.

Soar, golden eagle.

12 January – 12th Day of *Christmas*

Twelve drummers drumming

Pa-ra-pa-pam-pam. Peace on

Earth. First snow falls soft.

ABOUT THE AUTHOR

Patricia Furstenberg came to writing though reading, her passion for books being something she inherited from her parents. She is a skilled children's book author, poetess and mother, known for her uplifting, charming themes and lovable, enchanting characters. Her words "truly make the world a happier and more beautiful place!"

Patricia enjoys writing about animals because she believes that each animal, no matter how small, has a story to tell if you only stop to listen.

She lives in sunny South Africa with her husband, children and their dogs.

Find more of Patricia's stories on her author page, Alluring Creations, http://alluringcreations.co.za/wp/

Printed in Great Britain
by Amazon